The Urbana Free Library

To renew: call **217-367-4057**
or go to **urbanafreelibrary.org**
and select **My Account**

CYCLES OF THE NIGHT SKY

by Angie Smibert

The Child's World®
childsworld.com

Published by The Child's World®
1980 Lookout Drive • Mankato, MN 56003-1705
800-599-READ • www.childsworld.com

ISBN 9781503828452
LCCN 2018944806

Printed in the United States of America
PAO2396

About the Author

Angie Smibert is the author of several young adult and middle-grade science fiction and fantasy novels. She was a writer at NASA's Kennedy Space Center for many years. She received NASA's prestigious Silver Snoopy as well as several other awards for her work.

Table of Contents

CHAPTER ONE

An Ever-Moving Sky

The night sky is always in motion. Go outside just after dark. On a clear night, the stars appear to rise in the east. Then they move slowly across the sky. By dawn, the stars set in the west. The moon and planets follow their own paths through the sky. Go outside a few months later. The night sky will look different. New patterns of stars, or constellations, will be visible. Each of the motions of the night sky follows a cycle.

Ancient people knew about these cycles. They used them to mark the passage of months and years. Before the early 1500s, most people thought the sun and stars moved around Earth. The ancient Greeks imagined Earth was inside a ball of stars. They called this the **celestial sphere**. **Astronomers** today still use the idea of the celestial sphere to find stars and galaxies in the sky.

People have been studying the night sky for centuries.

The Greeks thought the sphere rotated around Earth. But we know now that it's Earth that really moves. It spins on its **axis**. And at the same time, Earth **orbits** around the sun. The other planets also move around the sun, and the moon orbits around Earth. All of these motions create the cycles of the night sky. Today, understanding the night sky helps people spot celestial objects. It also helps people predict **eclipses**.

Earth is constantly moving around the sun.

CHAPTER TWO

The Yearly Path

From Earth, the moon, planets, and many stars in the night sky seem to follow the same yearly path across the sky. This path is called the **ecliptic**. It's an imaginary plane that traces the sun's journey around the celestial sphere every day. Every night, many stars and constellations appear to have moved a little along the ecliptic.

The lines going from Earth, through the sun, and into space create the ecliptic plane.

Ecliptic Plane

Earth's Orbit

Of course, it's really Earth following this path. Earth orbits around the sun once every year. Every day, Earth moves about 1.6 million miles (2.5 million km). This makes the stars and constellations along the ecliptic look like they're moving in the opposite direction of Earth's motion.

Twelve constellations along the ecliptic have a special name: the zodiac. These constellations are equally spaced around the night sky. Modern astronomers use these constellations to describe where objects are in the sky.

Some astronomers watch the night sky in buildings called observatories.

CHAPTER THREE

The Nightly Rotation

The sun appears to rise in the east and set in the west. At night, the stars appear to do the same. This happens because Earth rotates on its axis. It takes Earth about 24 hours to spin around its axis once.

Earth's axis is tilted. This means Earth leans to its side a bit. The tilt creates the seasons. For example, summer happens when either the Northern or Southern **Hemisphere** is positioned towards the sun. At night, Earth's tilt makes the constellations along the ecliptic appear higher in the summer and lower in the winter. So some constellations will only be visible during certain seasons.

When the Northern Hemisphere has summer, the Southern Hemisphere is experiencing winter.

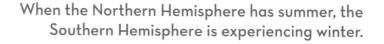

Summer

Winter

Equator

Sun

Earth's Wobble

Earth's spin has a wobble—much like a spinning top. Earth wobbles very slowly. Its poles move in a small circle that takes 25,800 years to draw. Today, Earth's north celestial pole points to Polaris. But 5,000 years ago, the pole pointed to the star Thuban. In 14,000 AD, the pole star will be Vega.

However, the constellations and stars directly overhead of the viewer are always visible. Ursa Minor, Cassiopeia, and Cepheus are examples of constellations in the Northern Hemisphere. These stars are near one of the celestial poles. The celestial poles are the points on the celestial sphere directly above the North and South Poles. The poles line up with Earth's axis. Stars appear to move around the poles. In the north, the celestial pole points to a pole star. The star is known as Polaris, or the North Star.

Telescopes help people see stars.

CHAPTER FOUR

Phases of the Moon

The moon has its own cycle in the night sky. The cycle lasts 29.5 days, or one **lunar** month. This is how long it takes for the moon to orbit Earth. At the beginning of the lunar month, people can't see the moon. But with each passing day, more and more of the moon is visible until it's full and round. And then people can see less and less of the moon until it disappears once again. These are the phases of the moon. Most calendar months are longer than a lunar month, so the phases of the moon may begin to repeat before the calendar month is completed.

The sun's light causes the moon to look different throughout the lunar month.

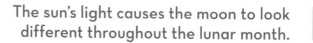

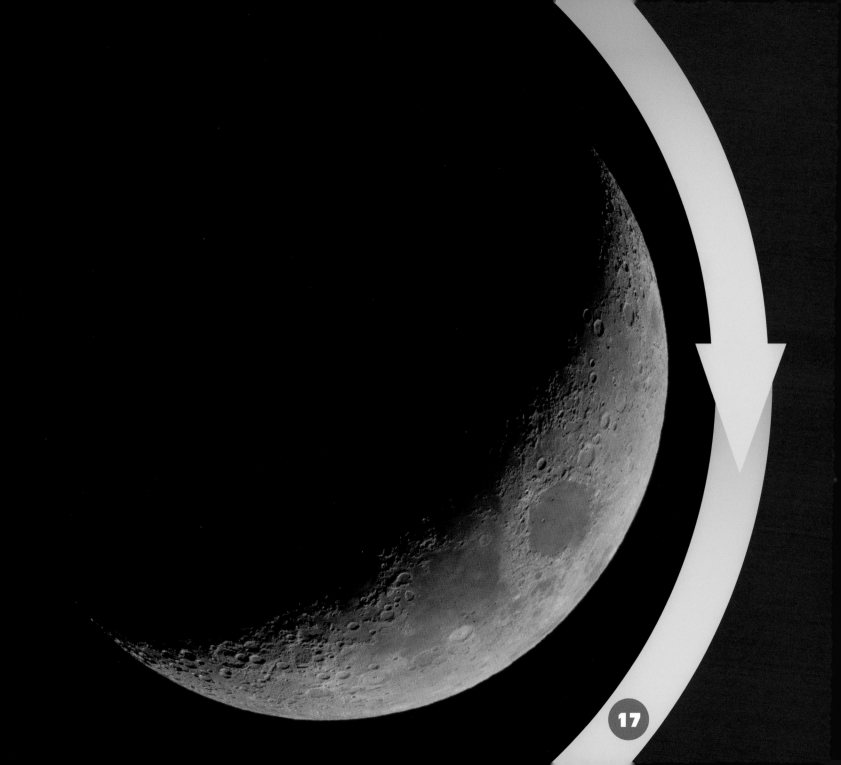

The phases are created by the moon orbiting Earth as Earth goes around the sun. The sun always lights up one-half of the moon. From Earth, though, people can't always see that lit half. What people see depends on where the moon is in its orbit. For instance, when the moon is between Earth and the sun, people can't see the lighted half of the moon at all. This phase is called the new moon. Two weeks later, the moon will be on the other side of Earth. All of the lighted surface will be visible. This is the full moon.

Sometimes, the sun, Earth, and the moon will line up perfectly, causing an eclipse. A lunar eclipse happens when the moon passes behind Earth and into Earth's shadow. A solar eclipse occurs when the moon passes between Earth and the sun, blocking the sun's light. A solar eclipse always happens at new moon, and a lunar eclipse always happens at full moon. However, solar and lunar eclipses don't happen at every new and full moon. That's because the moon, Earth, and the sun aren't perfectly lined up.

A total solar eclipse happens about every 18 months, but it's only visible in some areas on Earth.

Phases of the Moon as Seen from Earth

New Moon

Full Moon

The moon goes through eight phases during the lunar month. The different phases happen because of the moon's angle with the sun as seen from Earth.

Fast Facts

- The night sky has cycles that are caused by the motion of Earth and the moon.

- Earth orbits the sun once each year. Earth rotates on its axis once about every 24 hours.

- Ancient astronomers thought a celestial sphere of stars rotated around Earth. Modern astronomers still use the idea of the celestial sphere to locate objects in the sky.

- The ecliptic is the path the sun appears to take across the sky. The zodiac is the band of 12 constellations along the ecliptic.

- The phases of the moon depend on its position orbiting Earth.

- Eclipses happen when the moon's orbit lines up with Earth's at either the new moon or full moon.

Glossary

astronomers (uh-STRON-uh-merz) Astronomers study the stars, planets, and other objects in space. Astronomers discover new stars.

axis (AK-sis) An axis is a real or imaginary line through the center of an object, around which the object turns. Earth turns on its axis once a day.

celestial sphere (suh-LES-chuhl SFEER) The celestial sphere is an imaginary sphere of stars and other celestial objects that appears to rotate around Earth. Ancient astronomers thought Earth was surrounded by a celestial sphere.

eclipses (i-KLIPS-uz) Eclipses are when one celestial body covers another from the viewpoint of the observer. People on Earth can see both solar and lunar eclipses.

ecliptic (i-KLIP-tick) The ecliptic is the apparent path of the sun across the celestial sphere. The ecliptic is lower in the sky in the winter.

hemisphere (HEM-i-sfeer) A hemisphere is one-half of Earth. The Northern Hemisphere experiences summer from June through September.

lunar (LOO-nur) Lunar means having to do with the moon. The lunar month follows the moon's cycle.

orbits (OR-bitz) Orbits are the curved paths that something follows as it goes around something else. The moon orbits Earth.

To Learn More

IN THE LIBRARY

Hutmacher, Kimberly. *The Night Sky*.
Vero Beach, FL: Rourke Pub., 2013.

Schneider, Howard. *Night Sky*. Washington,
DC: National Geographic, 2016.

*Star Finder! A Step-by-Step Guide to the Night
Sky*. New York, NY: DK Publishing, 2017.

ON THE WEB

Visit our Web site for links about the cycles of the night sky:
childsworld.com/links

*Note to Parents, Teachers, and Librarians: We routinely verify our Web links to make
sure they are safe and active sites. So encourage your readers to check them out!*

Index